THE
Bon Appétit
KITCHEN
COLLECTION

Chocolate
Desserts

The Knapp Press
Publishers

Los Angeles

D0042766

Bon Appétit® is a registered trademark of
Bon Appétit Publishing Corp.
Used with permission.

Published by The Knapp Press
5900 Wilshire Boulevard, Los Angeles,
California 90036

Library of Congress Cataloging in Publication
Data
Main entry under title:

Chocolate desserts.

    (The Bon appétit kitchen collection)
    Includes index.
    1. Cookery (Chocolate) 2. Desserts.
    I. Series.
TX767.C5C49 1983   641.8'6   83-13617
ISBN 0-89535-125-0

Printed and bound in the United States of
America

On the cover: *Festive Chocolate Cookie Roll*

Photograph by Irwin Horowitz

Contents

1

Mousses, Puddings and Soufflés

Quick and Easy Chocolate Mousse

4 to 6 servings

- 12 ounces (2 cups) semisweet chocolate chips
- 1½ teaspoons vanilla
  Pinch of salt
- 1½ cups whipping cream, heated to boiling point
- 6 egg yolks

- 2 egg whites
  Whipped cream (optional)

Combine chocolate, vanilla and salt in blender or processor fitted with Steel Knife and mix 30 seconds. Add boiling cream and continue mixing 30 seconds more or until chocolate is completely melted. Add yolks and mix about 5 seconds. Transfer to bowl and allow to cool.

Beat egg whites until stiff peaks form. Gently fold into chocolate mixture. Place in serving bowl or wine glasses, cover with plastic wrap and chill. Serve with whipped cream if desired.

Chocolate Mousse au Provence

8 to 10 servings

- 6 ounces semisweet chocolate
- 2 ounces unsweetened chocolate
- 2 cups whipping cream
- 7 egg whites, room temperature
- 1 cup superfine sugar
- 7 dried jumbo apricots, finely chopped

2 teaspoons grated orange rind

1½ teaspoons instant coffee powder

Peppermint-Chocolate Leaves (see following recipe)

Place semisweet and unsweetened chocolate in top of double boiler over hot water until just softened (chocolate must not be hot). Whip cream until it begins to thicken. Add softened chocolate and continue whipping until stiff.

Whip egg whites until they form soft peaks. Gradually add sugar and beat until stiff. Fold into chocolate mixture. Carefully fold in apricots, orange rind and coffee powder.

Spoon into individual souffle dishes or custard cups and chill at least 4 hours. Arrange Peppermint-Chocolate Leaves on top just before serving.

Peppermint-Chocolate Leaves

- 3 ounces semisweet chocolate
- 3 drops peppermint extract
  Camellia leaves or any small, shiny leaves

Melt chocolate; add peppermint extract and mix thoroughly. Wash and dry leaves. Brush chocolate on shiny side of leaves, being careful to avoid getting chocolate on opposite side. Place on baking sheet lined with waxed paper and refrigerate until chocolate is set. Carefully peel leaf from chocolate. (If hands are warm, use tissue to hold leaf while removing chocolate in order to prevent melting.) Refrigerate until ready to serve. *Can be stored in refrigerator several weeks.*

Coco-Amaretto Mousse

6 servings

Coconut-Chocolate Crust

- 2 cups sweetened flaked coconut

- 6 ounces semisweet chocolate chips
- 2 tablespoons (¼ stick) unsalted butter
- 1 tablespoon light corn syrup

Chocolate Cigars

- 6 ounces semisweet chocolate chips

Almond Mousse Filling

- ¼ cup amaretto
- 2 teaspoons unflavored gelatin
- ½ cup sour cream, room temperature
- 1½ cups whipping cream
- 1 cup powdered sugar
- ¾ cup lightly toasted finely ground almonds

Chopped toasted almonds (optional garnish)

For crust, lightly grease 9- to 10-inch pie pan or deep square serving dish. Place coconut in medium bowl and warm in 150°F oven.

Combine chocolate chips, butter and corn syrup in top of double boiler over hot, not simmering, water. Stir until melted and smooth. Pour chocolate over warmed coconut and mix with 2 forks until thoroughly blended. Press coconut mixture evenly into bottom and sides of pie pan or dish. Chill.

For chocolate cigars, melt chocolate in top of double boiler over hot water, stirring until smooth. Spread chocolate over back of baking sheet into 4 × 6-inch rectangle. Cool to room temperature (65°F to 70°F) or refrigerate to firm, but chocolate must be room temperature to shape. Using cheese-shaver server (wire cheese cutter will not work), start an inch from short end of chocolate and pull server toward you in slightly upward motion so that chocolate will curl up and around. Use fingers to aid curling if necessary. Wrap cigars in plastic and refrigerate.

For filling, combine ¼ cup amaretto with gelatin in small, heat-resistant cup and mix until softened. Place cup in simmering water and heat until gelatin is completely liquefied, about 2 to 3 minutes. Transfer gelatin to large bowl. Add sour cream, blending well. Stir in cream and powdered sugar. Whip until stiff. Fold in almonds and spoon into shell. Decorate with chocolate cigars and chopped toasted almonds, if desired. Refrigerate until set, at least 2 hours.

Pots de Crème au Chocolat

This favorite of chocolate lovers everywhere loses nothing here in a lower-calorie translation.

8 servings

- 1 6-ounce package semisweet chocolate chips
- 2 large eggs

2 tablespoons very
   strongly brewed coffee
1 teaspoon rum extract
1 tablespoon orange
   liqueur
¾ cup scalded nonfat milk

Place chocolate chips, eggs, coffee, rum extract and orange liqueur in blender and whirl about 30 seconds. Add ¾ cup *hot* scalded nonfat milk and whirl again. Pour into 8 pots de crème cups, custard cups or Chinese teacups and chill.

Pots de Crème Turinois

Chestnut puree enhances the flavor of a traditional favorite.

10 to 12 servings

5 egg yolks
1½ cups whipping cream
1 cup milk
5 tablespoons sugar
2 tablespoons rum
½ cup unsweetened
   chestnut puree, mashed
   with fork to soften

4 ounces semisweet
chocolate, melted and
cooled

Whipped cream and
shaved chocolate
(garnish)

Preheat oven to 325°F. Beat egg
yolks until thick and lemon colored. Blend in cream and milk
and mix well. Add sugar, rum
and chestnut puree and beat
until blended. Add melted
chocolate and beat until smooth.
Pour into pots de crème cups,
3-ounce soufflé dishes or demi-
tasse cups. Set in shallow pan
and add hot water to come halfway up sides of cups. Bake until
just firm to the touch, about 45
to 60 minutes. Remove from
water bath and let cool to room
temperature. Garnish with
whipped cream rosettes and
shaved chocolate.

Pudding Malgache

An appealingly light substitute for chocolate soufflé, this dessert can be made two days in advance.

8 to 10 servings

- 1¼ cups milk
- 1½ ounces semisweet chocolate
- 6 tablespoons (¾ stick) unsalted butter, room temperature
- ⅔ cup all purpose flour
- ⅓ cup sugar
- 4 egg yolks, lightly beaten
- 3 egg whites

Ganache
- ½ cup whipping cream
- 4½ ounces semisweet chocolate

Preheat oven to 375°F. Butter 1½-quart soufflé dish. Combine milk and chocolate in 2-quart saucepan. Bring to boil over medium heat, stirring frequently.

Meanwhile, cream butter, flour and sugar in medium bowl (mixture will be very stiff). Add boiling milk and chocolate and blend well. Return to saucepan and cook, stirring constantly, until thickened. Remove from heat and beat small amount of hot mixture into egg yolks. Return to pan and beat well.

Beat whites until stiff but not dry. *Stir* into pudding mixture. Turn into soufflé dish; set in large pan and add hot water to a depth of about 2 inches. Bake until firm, about 40 minutes. Remove from water bath and let dish cool before unmolding.

For ganache, bring cream to boil in small saucepan. Remove from heat, add chocolate and beat until cool.

Unmold pudding onto rack. Reheat ganache slightly and spread over top of pudding. Transfer to serving plate and cut into wedges with hot knife.

Steamed Chocolate Pudding

2 servings

- 2 slices firm bread (preferably homemade), crusts trimmed
- ¼ cup whipping cream
- 3 tablespoons butter
- 1 egg
- 1 egg yolk
- 6 tablespoons powdered sugar
- 2 tablespoons melted chocolate chips or semisweet chocolate
- 2 tablespoons ground almonds
- ¼ teaspoon almond extract

  Boiling water
  Powdered sugar
  Unsweetened whipped cream (garnish)

Generously butter 2-cup mold and a piece of waxed paper or foil. Break bread into small pieces and transfer to small bowl. Add cream and beat until liquid is absorbed. Cream butter in large bowl using high speed of electric mixer until fluffy, about 5 minutes. Add bread and continue beating until light. Lightly beat egg with yolk in small bowl. Add to bread mixture alternately with sugar, beating well after each addition. Blend in chocolate, almonds and extract and mix thoroughly.

Turn mixture into mold. Cover with buttered paper or foil and tie securely over top of mold. Set on rack in steamer (or use cake cooling rack set into large saucepan) and pour in boiling water just to bottom of rack. Cover and steam over medium heat 2 hours, checking every 10 minutes to see if more boiling water needs to be added. Remove mold from steamer. Discard paper or foil. Let pudding cool 5 minutes. Invert onto serving platter. Dust with powdered sugar and garnish with cream.

Chocolate Soufflé

6 to 8 servings

- 1¼ cups half and half
- 6 ounces semisweet chocolate, cut into 1-inch pieces
- ¼ cup strongly brewed coffee

- 3 tablespoons butter
- 3 tablespoons all purpose flour
- 1 vanilla bean, split

- 4 egg yolks
- ¼ cup sugar

- 6 egg whites
- ¼ teaspoon salt
- ¼ teaspoon cream of tartar
  Powdered sugar

  Sweetened whipped cream, Crème à l'Anglaise (see recipe page 24) or softened vanilla ice cream mixed with a little whipped cream (garnish)

Oil inside of 1½-quart soufflé dish and dust lightly with sugar. Cut piece of waxed paper large enough to encircle dish with 2-

inch overlap and fold in half lengthwise. Grease upper half of paper and sprinkle with sugar. Wrap around outside of dish, allowing paper to extend 2 inches above rim; secure with string.

Combine half and half, chocolate and coffee in medium saucepan. Place over low heat and cook, stirring, until chocolate has melted. Set aside.

Melt butter in 2-quart saucepan over medium heat. Add flour and stir until bubbly. Whisking constantly, gradually add chocolate mixture. Continue cooking until thickened, about 3 to 4 minutes. Scrape soft inside of vanilla bean into mixture, then remove from heat.

Arrange rack in lower third of oven and preheat to 400°F. Beat yolks with 3 tablespoons sugar (reserve 1 tablespoon for whites) until light. Add a little of the chocolate mixture to yolks and blend well, then pour back into saucepan with remaining chocolate and blend thoroughly. Place over low heat and cook 1 minute, stirring constantly.

Transfer to 3- to 4-quart bowl and cool to room temperature.

In separate bowl, beat whites until foamy. Add salt and cream of tartar and beat until soft peaks form. Add remaining sugar and continue beating until stiff but not dry. Stir large spoonful of whites into chocolate mixture, then carefully fold in remaining whites. Gently spoon into prepared dish. Place in oven and immediately reduce temperature to 375°F. Bake 45 to 50 minutes or until cake tester inserted near center of soufflé comes out clean. Dust lightly with powdered sugar.

Take soufflé immediately to table with collar on. Remove string and waxed paper. Using 2 serving spoons, scoop soufflé from center into individual dishes. Accompany with whipped cream, chilled Crème à l'Anglaise or vanilla ice cream softened and mixed with a little whipped cream.

If desired, make individual soufflés by dividing same batter among 8 half-cup ramekins, extending waxed paper collars 1 inch above rim. Bake 25 to 30 minutes or until soufflés test done. Serve immediately.

Chocolate Tortoni

6 to 8 servings

    4 egg whites, room
      temperature
  ⅛ teaspoon cream of tartar
  ⅛ teaspoon salt
  ¼ cup sugar

    2 ounces unsweetened
      chocolate
    2 cups whipping cream
    2 teaspoons sugar
    1 tablespoon vanilla

    1 cup (6 ounces)
      semisweet chocolate
      chips
  ½ cup toasted slivered
      almonds
    2 tablespoons chopped
      candied cherries
      Whipped cream
      (optional)

Beat egg whites in large bowl until foamy. Add cream of tartar and salt and continue beating until soft peaks form. Beat in ¼ cup sugar 1 tablespoon at a time until mixture is stiff and shiny.

Melt unsweetened chocolate in top of double boiler over hot, not boiling, water. Beat whipping cream until thick, then beat in 2 teaspoons sugar, vanilla and melted chocolate and blend thoroughly. Fold in egg whites. Pour into freezerproof bowl and freeze until icy crystals form.

Melt chocolate chips in top of double boiler over hot water. Stir in almonds and cherries. Immediately fold into icy mixture and blend gently but thoroughly (small chunks of chocolate will form). Transfer to serving bowl or individual dishes and refreeze. Serve directly from bowl or dishes, or form into balls. Pass additional whipped cream if desired.

2

Crepes and Profiteroles

Sweet Crepes with Chocolate Topping

Makes about 2 dozen (8 to 12 servings)

Crepes
 1 cup all purpose flour
 2 tablespoons sugar
 3 eggs
 2 egg yolks
 1¾ cups plus 2 tablespoons milk
 2 tablespoons Cognac or brandy
 1 tablespoon finely grated orange or lemon peel
 Pinch of salt

3 tablespoons butter,
melted and clarified

Topping
4 ounces semisweet
chocolate, grated
1 tablespoon sugar
2 tablespoons (¼ stick)
unsalted butter, cut into
pieces

For crepes, combine flour and sugar in large bowl. Make well in center. Add eggs, yolks and ½ cup milk to bowl, whisking flour in slowly until mixture is smooth and shiny. Gradually whisk in remaining milk with Cognac. Stir in peel and salt. Let rest at room temperature about 2 hours. *(Batter can be prepared 2 days ahead and refrigerated.)*

Heat crepe pan over medium-high heat. Remove from heat and brush with some of clarified butter. Return to heat; sprinkle with small amount of water. If beads "dance" on pan, it is ready. Remove pan from heat. Working quickly, add about 3 table-spoons batter to one edge of pan, tilting and swirling until bottom is covered with thin layer of batter; pour any excess batter back into bowl.

Return pan to medium-high heat. Loosen edges of crepe with small spatula or knife, discarding any pieces of crepe clinging to sides of pan. Cook crepe until bottom is brown. Turn (or flip) crepe over and cook second side until brown. Slide out onto plate. Top with sheet of waxed paper or foil. Repeat with remaining batter, stirring occasionally and adjusting heat and adding more clarified butter to crepe pan or skillet as necessary.

To assemble, preheat oven to 350°F. Generously butter large round or square baking dish. Fold each crepe in half and then in half again to form triangle. Arrange in single layer in prepared dish, overlapping slightly. Sprinkle with chocolate and sugar. Dot with butter. Bake until chocolate is melted and crepes are heated through, about 20 minutes.

For Chocolate Crepes, prepare batter for Sweet Crepes in processor or blender, substituting ¼ cup unsweetened cocoa for ¼ cup flour. Use rum, coffee liqueur or crème de cacao instead of Cognac. Fill with chocolate mousse, bavarian cream or soufflé. Top with powdered sugar and whipped cream. (Chocolate Crepes should be made thicker than standard recipe.)

Frozen Chocolate Crepes

Makes 12

- 1 cup milk
- ½ cup all purpose flour
- ¼ cup sugar
- 2 eggs
- 2 tablespoons unsweetened cocoa
- 1 tablespoon butter, melted
- 1 teaspoon vanilla

    Butter

    Quick and Easy Chocolate Mousse (see recipe page 1)

    Crème à l'Anglaise (see following recipe)

With blender (do not use food processor): Combine first 7 in-

gredients and mix on low speed
about 30 seconds just until
combined; do not overblend.

With electric mixer: Combine
eggs and flour. Add sugar and
cocoa. Pour in milk gradually, beating continuously and
scraping sides of bowl to blend.
Add butter and vanilla and beat
until well mixed.

Allow batter to stand covered 1
hour before making crepes.

Place 8-inch crepe pan or skillet
over high heat and brush lightly
with butter. When butter is siz-
zling but not brown, pour about
¼ cup batter into pan. Quickly
lift pan off heat and swirl to coat
bottom and sides, pouring excess batter back into bowl. Return to heat and cook about 1
minute or until bottom darkens
slightly and looks dry. *Watch
carefully, since both cocoa and
sugar can cause crepes to burn
easily.* Turn crepe onto paper
towel or waxed paper. Continue
until all batter is used, brushing
pan with butter as needed.

When crepes have cooled, place
about 1 heaping tablespoon

mousse on each and roll cigar fashion. Place seam side down on baking sheet and freeze. When firm, wrap carefully and keep in freezer until serving.

To serve, place 1 or 2 crepes on each plate and spoon warmed Crème à l'Anglaise over.

Filled crepes may be wrapped and frozen up to 1 month.

Chocolate crepes may also be filled with flavored whipped cream and served with warm chocolate sauce.

Vanilla Custard Sauce (Crème à l'Anglaise)

      4 egg yolks
     ½ cup sugar
      1 vanilla bean, split
     1½ cups half and half

Combine yolks and sugar in small bowl. With point of sharp knife, scrape soft inside of vanilla bean into yolk mixture, reserving pod. Beat until light and fluffy. Place half and half and vanilla bean pod in 2-quart saucepan. Bring to boil over high heat, then remove pod. Beating constantly, very slowly pour hot half

and half into yolk mixture.
Transfer to saucepan and stir
constantly over low heat about
20 minutes or until custard coats
back of metal spoon. Serve warm
over crepes.

*Crème à l'Anglaise may be re-
heated in top of double boiler.
Place over hot water and beat
constantly.*

Profiteroles in Chocolate Sauce

Makes 5 to 6 dozen

   1 recipe Basic Choux
      Pastry (see following
      recipes)

   2 cups whipping cream
   6 tablespoons sugar
      (vanilla flavored
      preferred*)
   1 teaspoon vanilla
      Rich Thick Chocolate
      Sauce (see following
      recipes)

*Place about 4 cups sugar in 1-quart con-
tainer. Split 1 vanilla bean down center, ex-
posing seeds, and add to sugar. Let stand
1 week or longer to develop flavor.

¼ cup toasted slivered almonds (garnish)

Prepare and pipe out choux pastry in ¾-inch puffs (small size) and bake according to basic recipe directions. Cool completely on wire racks.

Whip cream with sugar and vanilla until stiff. Place cream in pastry tube and pipe into holes made in bottom of each puff; or remove tops from puffs, fill with cream and replace tops. Heap filled puffs in serving dish and pour chocolate sauce over. Garnish with almonds. Serve immediately.

Profiteroles may also be filled with vanilla ice cream and frozen until serving time.

Basic Choux Pastry

Makes 5 to 6 dozen profiteroles (small puffs)

  1 cup water
  ½ cup (1 stick) butter, cut into pieces
  1 cup all purpose flour
  ¼ teaspoon salt
  4 large eggs

Combine water and butter in heavy saucepan. Place over medium heat and cook until butter is melted and water comes to boil. Reduce heat to low, add flour and salt all at once and stir vigorously with wooden spoon until mixture is smooth and leaves sides of pan forming a ball, about 1 minute. Transfer mixture to bowl of electric mixer, or use hand mixer, and add eggs 1 at a time, beating well after each addition, until smooth and well blended. Cover lightly and let stand until completely cool.

Grease baking sheets liberally. Place dough in bag fitted with ½- to ⅝-inch plain round tip, or drop by teaspoonfuls onto prepared sheets, making ¾-inch mounds for small puffs. Use dull knife or small spatula dipped in cold water to separate dough from tip. Leave at least 1½ inches between puffs. Use dull knife or spatula to cut off tip of pastry, which tends to burn.

Preheat oven to 425°F. If time allows, refrigerate puffs on baking sheet 30 minutes or place in freezer 15 minutes; transfer directly to preheated oven (this will give a higher rise). Bake until golden brown and crusty, 18 to 20 minutes.

Remove baking sheets and turn off oven. Pierce side of each puff with sharp knife. Return to oven, leave door ajar, and let stand about 10 minutes to dry interior of puffs. Transfer to racks and let cool away from drafts.

Puffs may be frozen. Reheat, without thawing, in 375°F oven for 10 to 15 minutes.

Rich Thick Chocolate Sauce

    2 ounces unsweetened chocolate, cut into small pieces
    ½ cup sugar
    6 tablespoons (about) hot milk or cream
    ½ teaspoon vanilla
       Pinch of salt

Combine all ingredients in blender or food processor and whirl until smooth, adding more milk or cream until sauce reaches desired thickness.

3

Pies and Cheesecakes

Chocolate Mousse Pie

Chocolate cookie crumb crust enriches this easy-to-make but dramatic dessert.

10 to 12 servings

Crust
- 3 cups chocolate wafer crumbs
- ½ cup (1 stick) unsalted butter, melted

Filling
- 1 pound semisweet chocolate
- 2 eggs
- 4 egg yolks
- 2 cups (1 pint) whipping cream

   6 tablespoons powdered
       sugar
   4 egg whites, room
       temperature

Chocolate Leaves
   8 ounces (about)
       semisweet chocolate
   1 scant tablespoon
       vegetable shortening
       Camellia or other waxy
       leaves

   2 cups whipping cream
       Sugar

For crust, combine crumbs and
butter. Press on bottom and
completely up sides of 10-inch
springform pan. Refrigerate 30
minutes or chill in freezer.

For filling, soften chocolate in
top of double boiler over simmering water. Let cool to luke-
warm (95°F). Add whole eggs and
mix well. Add yolks and mix until thoroughly blended.

Whip cream with powdered
sugar until soft peaks form. Beat
egg whites until stiff but not dry.
Stir a little of the cream and
whites into chocolate mixture
to lighten. Fold in remaining

cream and whites until completely incorporated. Turn into crust and chill at least 6 hours, preferably overnight.

For leaves, melt chocolate and shortening in top of double boiler. Using spoon, generously coat underside of leaves. Chill or freeze until firm.

Whip remaining 2 cups cream with sugar to taste until stiff.

Loosen crust on all sides using sharp knife; remove springform. Spread all but about ½ cup cream over top of mousse. Pipe remaining cream into rosettes in center of pie.

Separate chocolate from leaves, starting at stem end of leaf. Arrange in overlapping pattern around rosettes. Cut pie into wedges with thin sharp knife.

Pie can be prepared ahead and frozen. Thaw overnight in the refrigerator before serving.

Chocolate Coffee Pie with Almond Crust

8 servings

Crust

- 2 egg whites
- ⅛ teaspoon (scant) cream of tartar
- ½ cup sugar
- 1½ cups (6 ounces) finely chopped blanched almonds

Filling

- 1 cup sugar
- 1 envelope unflavored gelatin
   Pinch of salt
- 2 eggs, separated
- 1 cup milk
- 1 12-ounce package semisweet chocolate chips
- ¼ cup coffee liqueur

- 1 cup whipping cream
- 1 teaspoon vanilla

For crust, preheat oven to 375°F. Beat egg whites until foamy. Add cream of tartar. Gradually add sugar and continue beating until stiff and glossy. Fold in almonds. Spread mixture over bottom and sides of an oiled 10-inch pie pan. Bake 15 to 20 minutes or until lightly browned. Set aside and let cool.

For filling, place ¼ cup sugar, gelatin and salt in top of double boiler. Beat together egg yolks and milk and add to gelatin. Cook over simmering water, stirring constantly, until slightly thickened. Add chocolate chips and continue cooking until chocolate has melted. Cool. Stir in coffee liqueur.

Beat egg whites until foamy. Slowly add ½ cup sugar and continue beating until whites are stiff and glossy. Fold into chocolate mixture.

Whip cream, adding final ¼ cup sugar and vanilla when cream is partially beaten. Spoon chocolate mixture and cream in alternating sections of cooled pie shell. Swirl with spoon to create marble effect. Chill until firm.

Mocha Pie

6 servings

- 1⅓ cups fine chocolate wafer crumbs (about 18 2¾-inch wafers)
- 3 tablespoons unsalted butter, room temperature

- 1 cup milk
- 3 tablespoons instant coffee powder
- 32 marshmallows

- 2 egg yolks

- 2 cups whipping cream

  Candy coffee beans or Chocolate Leaves (see following recipe) (garnish)

Preheat oven to 375°F. Crush or whirl chocolate wafers in blender or processor. Mash butter into crumbs. Press on bottom and sides of 8-inch pie pan. Bake for 8 minutes.

Over medium heat, combine milk and coffee powder in 3-quart saucepan. Stir to dissolve. Add marshmallows; heat until marshmallows are melted, stirring constantly.

Beat yolks until pale yellow. Add a few tablespoons marshmallow mixture to yolks; stir. Add to marshmallow mixture in pan; cook 1 minute, stirring constantly. Pour into 3-quart bowl. Refrigerate until thickened but not set.

Whip cream and fold 1 cup cream into marshmallow mixture. Pour into prepared crust. Chill until firm.

Use remaining whipped cream for garnish. Decorate with coffee beans or Chocolate Leaves.

Chocolate Leaves

> 1 ounce (1 square)
> unsweetened chocolate
> Mint leaves

Melt chocolate and brush underside of mint leaves. Freeze. When chocolate is firm, peel leaf from chocolate.

Unbelievable Pie

6 servings

- ½ cup coarsely chopped toasted nuts
- 1 unbaked 8-inch graham cracker crust

- 1 ounce semisweet chocolate
- ½ cup (1 stick) unsalted butter
- 1 cup sugar
- 2 eggs, well beaten
  Whipped cream or ice cream

Preheat oven to 350°F. Sprinkle nuts on bottom of pie shell and set aside.

Combine chocolate and butter in top of double boiler over gently simmering water. Whisk until melted and well blended. Remove from heat and whisk in sugar. Beat small amount of warmed chocolate into eggs. Add to chocolate mixture and blend well. Pour into pie shell (uncooked mixture will not fill shell) and bake until filling is puffed, about 25 minutes. Serve warm or at room temperature with whipped cream or your favorite ice cream.

Swiss Chocolate Almond Pie

8 servings

Crust
- 2 cups all purpose flour
- ¾ cup (1½ sticks) unsalted butter, cut into small pieces
- ¾ cup coarsely chopped sliced almonds
- ¼ cup firmly packed brown sugar
- 1 ounce semisweet chocolate (preferably Swiss), grated
- ¼ teaspoon salt
- 1 tablespoon Swiss chocolate almond liqueur
- ½ teaspoon almond extract
  Water

Filling
- ½ cup (1 stick) butter, room temperature
- ⅔ cup sugar

  2 ounces unsweetened
    chocolate, melted and
    cooled
  2 eggs
  1 tablespoon Swiss
    chocolate almond
    liqueur
  ½ teaspoon almond extract

Topping
  2 cups whipping cream
  ¼ cup powdered sugar
  2 tablespoons Swiss
    chocolate almond
    liqueur

For crust, preheat oven to 375°F. Generously grease 9-inch pie pan. Combine flour and butter in medium bowl and mix with fingertips until consistency of coarse meal. Gently blend in almonds, sugar, chocolate and salt. Remove ½ cup mixture for garnish. Sprinkle liqueur and almond extract over remaining mixture and toss together, adding water as needed, until dough can be formed into ball.

Press into bottom and sides of prepared pie pan. Bake until crust is set and almonds are browned, about 15 minutes.

Spread reserved mixture on baking sheet and bake until browned, about 5 minutes. Cool.

For filling, cream butter. Gradually add sugar and beat until mixture is light and fluffy. Stir in chocolate. Add eggs one at a time, beating well after each addition. Stir in liqueur and almond extract. Turn into prepared crust, spreading evenly. Refrigerate.

Shortly before serving, beat topping ingredients until stiff. Spoon into pastry bag fitted with large star tip and pipe over filling. Chop crumbs for garnish.

Bountiful Hot Fudge Sundae Pie

10 to 12 servings

Chocolate Cookie Crumb Crust
- 1¼ cups fine chocolate wafer crumbs
- ¼ cup finely ground toasted nuts (almonds, hazelnuts or walnuts)
- 3 tablespoons sugar

6 tablespoons (¾ stick)
unsalted butter, melted

Hot Fudge Sauce
1 cup sugar
¾ cup unsweetened cocoa,
sifted
1 teaspoon instant coffee
powder
1 cup whipping cream
¼ cup (½ stick) unsalted
butter

Filling
1 quart rich vanilla ice
cream, softened

1 quart rich chocolate ice
cream, frozen
½ cup whipping cream,
whipped
Coarsely chopped
toasted nuts (garnish)
Maraschino cherries
(with stems), rinsed and
drained (garnish)

For crust, combine crumbs, nuts
and sugar in small bowl and mix
well. Pour melted butter over
mixture and toss lightly until
well blended. Press mixture
evenly into bottom and up sides
of 9- to 10-inch pie pan. Cover

with plastic wrap and chill at least 30 minutes.

For sauce, combine sugar, cocoa and instant coffee in medium saucepan. Add ½ cup whipping cream and blend to smooth paste. Add remaining cream, blending well. Cook over medium heat, stirring constantly, until sugar is completely dissolved. Add butter and cook until mixture is smooth and thickened, about 5 to 8 minutes. Keep warm. *(Can be prepared ahead, covered and refrigerated. Reheat before using.)*

For filling, spread half of softened vanilla ice cream evenly over crust and freeze. Drizzle half of hot fudge sauce over top (fudge will solidify). Spread remaining vanilla ice cream over fudge. Return to freezer to firm.

Scoop balls from chocolate ice cream and arrange over vanilla layer. Drizzle with remaining hot fudge. Spoon whipped cream into pastry bag fitted with star tip and pipe rosettes around scoops. Garnish with nuts and cherries. Serve immediately.

Chocolate Cheesecake

8 to 10 servings

- 1 cup cottage cheese
- ½ cup sugar
- ½ cup chopped walnuts
- 2 egg yolks
- 1 teaspoon vanilla
- 8 ounces semisweet chocolate, melted
- 1 cup whipping cream, whipped
- 2 egg whites, stiffly beaten
- 1 9-inch graham cracker or cornflake crumb crust, baked

Whipped cream and walnut halves (garnish)

Combine first 5 ingredients in large mixing bowl and beat with electric mixer on high speed until smooth. Add chocolate and blend well. Fold in whipped cream, then egg whites. Fill crust, cover and refrigerate at least 24 hours. Garnish with whipped cream and walnuts just before serving.

Fudge Almond Cheesecake

Richly almond flavored, this cake is a perfect choice for marzipan lovers. For ease, it's made with a processor.

12 servings

- 1½ cups gingersnap crumbs
- ¼ cup (½ stick) melted butter

- 3 8-ounce packages (1½ pounds) cream cheese, cut into chunks
- 1 cup sugar
- 3 eggs
- 2 teaspoons almond extract
- 2 teaspoons vanilla

- 1 6-ounce package semisweet chocolate chips
- 3 tablespoons butter

  Chocolate curls (optional garnish)

Preheat oven to 350°F. Place gingersnaps in processor. Process with double Steel Knife, using an on/off motion, until fine crumbs are formed. Add melted butter and process a few seconds more. Press crumbs evenly into bottom of 9-inch springform pan.

Wipe out plastic bowl. Using double Steel Knife, add cream cheese. Process until smooth, using on/off motion. Add sugar, eggs and extracts. Process until well blended, 15 to 20 seconds.

Pour into pan. Bake 45 minutes. Turn off oven. Allow cake to cool in oven with door open. When cool, carefully remove from pan.

Melt chocolate and butter together. Swirl over top of cooled cake. Garnish generously with large chocolate curls if desired.

4

Cakes and Tortes

Best Chocolate Cake

24 to 30 servings

- 2 cups sugar
- 2 cups all purpose flour
- ¼ cup unsweetened cocoa
- ½ cup (1 stick) butter
- 1 cup water
- ½ cup oil
- 2 eggs
- ½ cup buttermilk
- 1½ teaspoons baking soda
- 1 teaspoon vanilla

- 1 16-ounce box powdered sugar
- 1 cup toasted chopped nuts

¼ cup unsweetened cocoa

½ cup (1 stick) butter

⅓ cup buttermilk

1 teaspoon vanilla

Preheat oven to 350°F. Combine first 3 ingredients in large bowl. Melt butter with water and oil in small saucepan over medium-high heat and bring to boil. Pour over dry ingredients and mix well. Add eggs, ½ cup buttermilk, baking soda and 1 teaspoon vanilla and blend thoroughly. Pour into 18 × 11-inch rectangular roasting pan. Bake until tester inserted in center of cake comes out clean, approximately 20 to 25 minutes.

Meanwhile, combine powdered sugar, nuts and remaining cocoa in mixing bowl.

Remove cake from oven. Melt remaining butter in small saucepan over medium heat. Add to sugar mixture with remaining buttermilk and vanilla and blend thoroughly. Immediately pour over cake, spreading evenly to edges. Let cake cool completely in pan.

Mocha Bundt Cake

12 to 15 servings

- 1 package white cake mix
- 1 3¾-ounce package instant chocolate pudding mix
- 4 eggs
- 1 cup oil
- ⅔ cup vodka
- ⅓ cup coffee liqueur
- ¼ cup water
- ¼ cup coffee liqueur
- ¼ cup powdered sugar

Preheat oven to 350°F. Grease and flour bundt cake pan, shaking out excess. Combine first 7 ingredients in large bowl and beat thoroughly. Pour into pan. Bake until tester inserted in center comes out clean, about 50 to 60 minutes. Let cool 5 minutes in pan, then invert onto rack. Blend ¼ cup coffee liqueur with powdered sugar in small bowl until smooth. Drizzle evenly over warm cake.

Queen of Sheba Cake

An easily made cake that's good for a crowd.

16 servings

Cake
- ½ cup (1 stick) unsalted butter, room temperature
- ½ cup sugar
- 3 egg yolks
- 7 ounces semisweet chocolate, melted and cooled
- 2 tablespoons finely ground almonds
- 2 tablespoons dark rum *or* coffee liqueur
- ⅛ teaspoon almond extract

- ⅔ cup all purpose flour
- 1 teaspoon baking powder
  Generous pinch of salt

- 4 egg whites
- 2 tablespoons sugar

Glaze
- 8 ounces semisweet chocolate, cut into pieces
- ½ cup (1 stick) unsalted butter, cut into pieces
- 4 teaspoons honey

Buttercream
- ¼ cup unsweetened cocoa
- ¼ cup milk
- 2½ tablespoons unsalted butter
- 2½ tablespoons vegetable shortening
- ½ teaspoon vanilla
  Pinch of salt
- ½ pound (about) powdered sugar, sifted

  Candy coffee beans (garnish)

For cake, preheat oven to 400°F. Butter 8-inch round cake pan and line bottom with parchment paper; set aside.

Beat butter in large mixing bowl until fluffy. Gradually add ½ cup sugar and beat on high speed 7 to 8 minutes. Add yolks and beat well. Stir in chocolate, almonds, rum and almond extract.

Sift together next 3 ingredients. Return to sifter and set aside.

Beat egg whites in large bowl until soft peaks form. Add sugar 1 tablespoon at a time and beat until stiff.

Sift ⅓ of flour mixture over batter. Add ⅓ of whites and fold gently. Repeat, beating whites quickly just before adding. Repeat with remaining flour and whites and fold thoroughly. Turn mixture into prepared pan, spreading evenly.

Bake 15 to 18 minutes (1½ inches along outer edge of cake should be done, but center should still be uncooked.) Set on rack and let cool in pan 1 to 2 hours. (Cake will sink in center; push outer edge down occasionally to make it as even with middle as possible.) Chill cake at least 6 hours, preferably overnight, before unmolding from pan.

For glaze, combine chocolate, butter and honey in top of double boiler and melt over hot, not boiling, water, stirring occasionally until smooth. Remove and let cool to about 100°F.

While glaze cools, remove cake from refrigerator and unmold. Using sharp knife, trim any higher outer edges to make cake a little more level (it will still be lower in center).

Cut out 8-inch circle of cardboard and set cake on top. Place on rack over baking sheet. Stir glaze gently with rubber spatula (be careful not to make air bubbles). Pour glaze onto center of cake, tilting rack so glaze coats top and sides of cake completely. Refrigerate immediately to set glaze, 2 to 3 hours. *(Cake can be prepared 1 day ahead to this point; cover with plastic after glaze sets.)*

For buttercream, combine cocoa, milk, butter, shortening, vanilla and salt in small bowl and blend well. Beat in powdered sugar 1 tablespoon at a time until mixture is stiff enough to be piped. Spoon into pastry bag fitted with star tip and pipe 8 rosettes around outer edge of cake and 1 in center. Set coffee bean in center of each. Refrigerate until ready to serve.

Chocolate Upside Down Cake

8 to 10 servings

- ¾ cup (1½ sticks) butter, room temperature
- ½ cup firmly packed brown sugar
- ½ cup light corn syrup
- ½ cup chopped nuts

- 1 cup sugar
- 1 egg, separated
- 2 ounces unsweetened chocolate, melted and cooled
- 1¼ cups all purpose flour
- 1 teaspoon baking powder
- ¼ teaspoon salt
- ¾ cup milk
- 1 teaspoon vanilla

Preheat oven to 350°F. Grease 10-inch tube pan with vegetable shortening and line bottom with waxed paper. Cream ½ cup butter and brown sugar in medium mixing bowl. Add syrup and nuts and mix well. Spread evenly on bottom of pan.

In large mixing bowl, thoroughly cream remaining butter and sugar. Beat in egg yolk and chocolate. Sift together flour, baking powder and salt and beat in alternately with milk and vanilla. Beat egg white in separate bowl until it holds stiff peaks. Fold into batter. Turn into pan and bake 45 to 50 minutes. Let cool 10 minutes, turn pan over onto plate and let stand 10 minutes more before removing pan. *If some of candy mixture sticks, it can be easily pressed onto cake.*

French Chocolate Cake with Chocolate Glaze

The center of this cake is not thoroughly cooked by American standards; hence its soft texture and distinctive flavor.

6 to 8 servings

- 1 cup (5½ ounces) unblanched almonds

- 4 ounces semisweet chocolate or ¾ cup semisweet chocolate chips

½ cup (1 stick) butter,
room temperature, cut
into pieces

⅔ cup sugar

3 eggs
Grated rind of 1 large
orange

¼ cup very fine dry
breadcrumbs

Chocolate Glaze (see
following recipe)

Butter sides of 8-inch round
cake pan. Line bottom with
kitchen parchment. Set aside.

Grind almonds as fine as possible in food processor or
blender. Set aside.

Preheat oven to 375°F. Melt
chocolate in top of a double
boiler over hot, *not boiling,* water.
Work butter with an electric
beater or in an electric mixer
until very soft and light. Gradually work in sugar, beating constantly. Add eggs, one at a time,
beating hard after each addition. (At this point, batter may
appear curdled.) Stir in melted
chocolate, ground nuts, orange
rind and breadcrumbs thoroughly. Pour into prepared pan

and bake for 25 minutes. Remove from oven and cool in pan for 30 minutes on a cake rack. Turn cake out onto rack. Lift off and discard parchment. Cool.

Chocolate Glaze

- 2 ounces unsweetened chocolate
- 2 ounces semisweet chocolate or ¼ cup semisweet chocolate chips
- ¼ cup (½ stick) butter, softened and cut into pieces
- 2 teaspoons honey

Toasted slivered almonds

Combine two chocolates, butter and honey in top of double boiler. Melt over hot water. Remove from heat and beat until it is cool but can still be poured.

Place cake on a rack over waxed paper and pour glaze over all. Tip cake so glaze runs evenly over top and down sides. Smooth sides, if necessary, with a metal spatula. Generously garland rim of cake with toasted slivered almonds, placing them close together.

This cake freezes successfully if wrapped and sealed securely. Bring to room temperature before serving and glaze will become shiny.

Festive Chocolate Cookie Roll

8 servings

Creamy Chocolate Frosting
>   1 cup semisweet chocolate chips
>   ⅔ cup firmly packed brown sugar
>   3 ounces cream cheese, room temperature
>   ½ teaspoon vanilla
>   ½ teaspoon cinnamon
>   Pinch of salt
>   1 egg yolk
>   1 cup whipping cream, whipped

Cake
>   ⅓ cup all purpose flour
>   ½ teaspoon baking powder
>   14 Oreo cookies, crushed
>   5 eggs, separated (room temperature)

½ cup sugar
1 teaspoon vanilla

2 tablespoons powdered
   sugar

Cream Filling
   1 cup whipping cream,
      whipped
   ½ cup slivered almonds,
      toasted
   ¼ teaspoon almond extract

   Meringue mushrooms
   (garnish)

For frosting, melt chocolate chips in small saucepan over low heat. Combine brown sugar, cream cheese, vanilla, cinnamon and salt in large bowl. Add yolk and beat until fluffy. Stir in chocolate; fold in whipped cream. Chill at least 1 to 1½ hours or overnight.

For cake, preheat oven to 350°F. Grease 10½ × 15½-inch jelly roll pan. Line pan with foil; lightly grease foil. Sift flour and baking powder into medium bowl. Stir in cookie crumbs and set aside. Beat yolks with sugar at medium speed in large bowl of electric mixer until just blended.

Stir in vanilla and set aside. Beat whites in another bowl until stiff. Stir ⅓ of crumbs into yolk mixture. Gently fold in ⅓ of whites. Repeat twice. Spread batter evenly into prepared pan. Bake until tester inserted in center comes out clean, approximately 15 minutes.

Sprinkle powdered sugar over towel. Remove cake from oven and cover pan with towel, sugar side down, then top with cutting board, if desired. Invert cake onto towel and board or other flat surface. Remove pan and gently peel off foil. Carefully roll up cake starting from short end, using towel as aid. Cool on rack 30 minutes.

For filling, combine whipped cream, almonds and almond extract in small bowl. Set aside.

To assemble, unroll cake and remove towel. Spread filling evenly, almost to edges of cake. Gently reroll cake. Transfer to serving platter. Spread frosting over top and ends. Make loglike marks using fork tines. Garnish with meringue mushrooms and refrigerate until ready to serve.

Petites Buches au Chocolat

These small chocolate rolls (or logs) are filled with walnut marzipan and crème chantilly, thinly frosted with chocolate icing and rolled in either walnuts or chocolate sprinkles.

24 to 26 servings

Chocolate Roll
- 6 ounces semisweet chocolate
- 3 tablespoons water

- 5 eggs, separated
- ¼ teaspoon cream of tartar
- ¾ cup sugar
- 1 teaspoon vanilla

Walnut Marzipan
- 12 ounces grated walnuts (3 cups)
- 8 ounces finely crushed vanilla wafers (2 cups)
- ⅔ cup powdered sugar (optional)
- ⅓ cup light corn syrup
- ⅓ cup dark rum or coffee liqueur
- 2½ tablespoons unsweetened cocoa

Crème Chantilly
- 1 cup whipping cream, well chilled
- ¼ cup powdered sugar
- 1 teaspoon vanilla

- ½ cup powdered sugar
- ¼ cup unsweetened cocoa

  Chocolate Icing (see following recipe)

- ½ cup toasted chopped walnuts or chocolate sprinkles (garnish)

For roll, preheat oven to 350°F. Butter 15½ × 1-inch jelly roll pan. Line with waxed paper, extending paper a few inches over each end; oil paper lightly.

Melt chocolate with water in top of double boiler over simmering water. Stir until smooth. Let cool.

Beat egg whites until foamy. Add cream of tartar and beat until soft peaks form. Gradually add half the sugar and beat until stiff but not dry. In large bowl combine egg yolks, remaining sugar and vanilla and beat until thick and pale yellow. Blend in chocolate; mix well.

Stir 2 large spoonfuls of whites into yolks and mix thoroughly. Gently fold in remaining whites; *do not overfold*. Turn into prepared pan, spreading evenly. Bake until edges of cake shrink slightly from pan, about 15 to 20 minutes. Cover cake with slightly dampened towel and let cool.

For marzipan, combine ingredients in processor or electric mixer fitted with paddle attachment; mix thoroughly. Roll between 2 sheets of waxed paper into same size as top of chocolate cake.

For crème, combine whipping cream, powdered sugar and vanilla in chilled mixing bowl and beat until thick. Cover and refrigerate.

Remove towel from cake. Combine powdered sugar and cocoa and sift over surface. Cover with 2 overlapping layers of waxed paper, place a board or bottom of another jelly roll pan on top and invert cake onto work surface. Gently peel off waxed paper.

Remove top layer of waxed paper from marzipan and invert over cake. Remove the other sheet of waxed paper. Spread crème over marzipan. Cut cake lengthwise into 2 halves. Roll long edge toward center to form long, thin cylinder. Wrap with plastic and place in freezer. Repeat with second half.

When solidly frozen, unwrap rolls and pour thin coating of Chocolate Icing slowly over tops, rotating to cover sides. Roll in chopped walnuts or sprinkles and chill to set the icing. Cut into 1-inch pieces and place each in decorative paper cup with a scalloped edge.

Chocolate Icing

- 2 cups powdered sugar
- ⅔ cup unsweetened cocoa
- 1 tablespoon vegetable oil
- 4 tablespoons (about) strongly brewed hot coffee

Combine sugar and cocoa and sift into bowl. Add oil and 2 tablespoons coffee and beat vigorously. Blend in additional coffee 1 teaspoon at a time until icing is thin enough to pour.

Chocolate Rum Charlotte

This rich dessert freezes to the consistency of a thick mousse.

10 servings

> Chocolate Cream (see following recipe)

6	ounces (about 18) ladyfingers, split
⅓	cup dark Jamaica rum (about)
½	cup whipping cream
1	tablespoon sugar
½	teaspoon vanilla
½	teaspoon dark Jamaica rum
3	tablespoons finely chopped pecans

Prepare Chocolate Cream.

Line bottom of unbuttered 2-quart charlotte mold* with circle of waxed paper. Trim enough ladyfingers into pointed-tip petal shapes to make a rosette pattern to line bottom of mold. Arrange, curved side down, in bottom of mold. Cut a small circle from 1 ladyfinger to form center of rosette and place in mold. Drizzle rosette with just enough rum to moisten.

Cut rounded tips off one end of enough additional ladyfingers to line inside of mold. Drizzle lightly with rum to moisten. Arrange vertically, trimmed ends down, with sides touching and rounded sides outward to line walls of mold. Fill with Chocolate Cream. Trim off any tips of ladyfingers extending above surface of filling. Arrange remaining ladyfinger pieces to cover filling and, if necessary, use additional ladyfingers moistened with rum to cover completely. Cover and freeze at least 8 hours.

*Traditional charlotte molds are available in well-stocked specialty cookware stores. A straight-sided pudding mold, soufflé dish or springform pan may be substituted.

Just before serving, lightly whip cream. Add sugar, vanilla and rum and beat until blended but not stiff. To serve, loosen charlotte at sides and turn out onto serving platter. Spoon puffs of whipped cream decoratively around base of charlotte and sprinkle cream with pecans. Cut into slender wedges and pass any remaining whipped cream.

Chocolate Cream

Makes about 4 cups

- 1 14-ounce can sweetened condensed milk
- 6 ounces semisweet chocolate
- 3 tablespoons dark Jamaica rum
- 1 cup whipping cream, whipped

Combine milk and chocolate in top of double boiler. Place over gently simmering water and stir constantly until chocolate is melted and mixture is smooth. Transfer to bowl and cool to room temperature, stirring occasionally. When cool, stir in rum. Gently fold in whipped cream until blended.

Chocolate Hazelnut Torte with Poached Pears

6 servings

Poached Pears

    2 cups water
    2 cups sugar
    3 1-inch strips lemon peel
    1 1-inch piece cinnamon
      stick
    1 1-inch piece vanilla bean,
      split, or 1 tablespoon
      vanilla

    3 large ripe pears
    ½ lemon

Chocolate Hazelnut Torte

    3 ounces bittersweet
      chocolate, coarsely
      chopped
    ¼ cup (½ stick) unsalted
      butter

    3 egg yolks, room
      temperature
    1 tablespoon pear liqueur

    3 egg whites, room
      temperature
      Pinch of salt
      Pinch of cream of tartar

½ cup (3 ounces) husked
hazelnuts, toasted and
ground

¼ cup all purpose flour,
sifted

Ganache

1½ cups whipping cream

15 ounces bittersweet
chocolate, coarsely
chopped

¼ cup (½ stick) unsalted
butter

2 tablespoons pear liqueur

¼ cup (1½ ounces) husked
hazelnuts, toasted and
chopped

½ cup whipping cream,
whipped

For pears, combine water, sugar,
lemon peel, cinnamon stick and
vanilla in heavy large saucepan.
Cook over low heat, swirling pan
occasionally, until sugar is dissolved. Increase heat and simmer gently for 10 minutes.

Peel pears; halve lengthwise and
rub with cut lemon (do not core).
Add to simmering liquid. Cover
and poach until tender, about
15 minutes, turning halfway

through cooking time. Let pears cool in poaching liquid.

For torte, preheat oven to 350°F. Line 8-inch round cake pan with circle of parchment paper. Butter and flour paper, shaking out excess. Bring water to boil in bottom of double boiler; turn off heat. Combine chocolate and butter in top of double boiler and stir until melted and smooth. Let cool.

Remove pears from poaching liquid using slotted spoon. Measure ⅓ cup liquid into medium mixing bowl; reserve remaining liquid. Add egg yolks and beat until thick and lemon colored, about 5 minutes. Gently stir in melted chocolate and 1 tablespoon liqueur.

Beat egg whites until foamy. Add salt and cream of tartar and continue beating until stiff but not dry. Combine ground hazelnuts and flour. Fold whites into yolks alternately with hazelnut mixture, ending with whites. Pour into prepared pan. Tap pan on counter to remove air bubbles. Bake until torte is puffed and tester inserted in center comes out clean, about 25 to 30 minutes. Let cool 10 minutes. Unmold; wrap in plastic bag and refrigerate.

For ganache, bring 1½ cups cream to boil in heavy saucepan. Remove from heat and add chocolate and butter; stir occasionally until melted and smooth. Strain into bowl. Stir in liqueur and 2 tablespoons poaching liquid. Refrigerate until thickened, 2 to 3 hours.

Place torte on work surface. Beat ⅓ of ganache in small bowl until fluffy. Spread over top and sides of torte. Core pears and pat dry with paper towels. Arrange on top of ganache cut side down with small ends facing center. Place torte on rack and set over jelly roll pan. Spoon remaining ⅔ of ganache over torte, covering completely. Transfer to serving plate. Decorate center with chopped hazelnuts and tiny rosettes of whipped cream. Chill several hours. Let stand at room temperature at least 30 minutes before serving.

Pears can be poached several days ahead and refrigerated in poaching liquid. Remaining poaching liquid can be frozen.

Mocha Brownie Torte

This dish should be made 1 or 2 days in advance.

16 servings

⅔ cup softened butter
⅓ cup sugar
4 egg yolks
3 ounces semisweet chocolate, grated

4 egg whites
1½ cups finely ground almonds

½ cup sifted all purpose flour
⅛ teaspoon baking powder

Coffee Cream Filling (see following recipes)

⅓ cup seedless raspberry jam
Chocolate Icing (see following recipes)

8 halved almonds (garnish)

Whipped cream
(optional)

Preheat oven to 350°F. Cream
butter and sugar, add egg yolks
and beat until light and fluffy.
Thoroughly blend in grated
chocolate.

Beat egg whites to soft peaks.
Gently fold into chocolate mixture with ground almonds.

Sift flour and baking powder together. Fold in gently but thoroughly. Pour batter into buttered
and floured 8 × 8 × 2-inch pan.
Bake until cake shrinks from
sides of pan, about 30 to 40 minutes. Cool and remove from pan.
Cover and refrigerate overnight.

Split cake in half horizontally;
place on serving plate. Spread
Coffee Cream Filling on bottom
layer. Cover with top layer. Wrap
and return to refrigerator for
several hours or overnight.

Coat top layer with raspberry
jam. Score cake into 16 even
squares without slicing completely through. Pour Chocolate
Icing over top and sides of cake,

using knife to cover sides completely. Refrigerate.

After icing is set, cut squares
through. Place a split almond in
center of each square. Refrigerate cake for at least 1 hour before serving. Decorate with a frill
of whipped cream if desired.

Coffee Cream Filling

   1 teaspoon instant coffee
     powder
   1 tablespoon hot water
  ¼ cup (½ stick) unsalted
     butter, room
     temperature
  ¼ cup sugar
   1 egg yolk

Dissolve coffee in hot water.
Cream butter and sugar together; add egg yolk and beat
thoroughly. Add coffee liquid.
Beat again until fluffy.

Chocolate Icing

   4 ounces semisweet
     chocolate
  ½ cup (1 stick) unsalted
     butter

Melt chocolate and butter over
low heat, stirring until smooth
and well blended. Cool slightly.

5

Cookies and Brownies

No-Bake Fudge Cookies

Makes about 4 dozen

- 2 cups sugar
- ½ cup milk
- ⅓ cup unsweetened cocoa
- ¼ cup (½ stick) butter, room temperature
- ¼ cup peanut butter
- 3 cups quick-cooking oats

Combine sugar, milk, cocoa and butter in medium saucepan. Place over medium-high heat and bring to boil, stirring constantly. Let boil 1 minute. Remove from heat. Mix in peanut butter. Add oats and blend thoroughly. Drop by teaspoonfuls onto waxed paper. Let cool completely. *Store cookies in airtight container.*

Chocolate Fudgy Brownies

Makes 16

- ½ cup (1 stick) butter
- 2 ounces unsweetened chocolate
- 1 cup sugar
- ½ cup all purpose flour
- ½ teaspoon baking powder
- 2 eggs
- 1 teaspoon vanilla
- ½ cup chopped walnuts

Preheat oven to 450°F. Grease an 8-inch square baking pan. Melt butter with chocolate in medium saucepan. Remove from heat. Combine sugar, flour and baking powder in large bowl. Add eggs and vanilla and beat well. Pour in chocolate mixture and blend thoroughly. Stir in walnuts. Pour into pan. Bake until tester inserted in center comes out clean, about 15 to 20 minutes. Cool completely in pan before cutting into squares.

Bittersweet Brownies

Makes about 40

- 1½ cups sifted all purpose flour
- ¾ cup plus 2 tablespoons unsweetened cocoa
- 1½ teaspoons salt
- 1 teaspoon baking powder
- 1⅓ cups butter
- 2 cups sugar
- 4 eggs
- ¼ cup light corn syrup
- 2 teaspoons vanilla
- 2 cups coarsely chopped toasted nuts

  Chocolate Frosting (see following recipe)

Preheat oven to 350°F. Grease 9 × 13-inch baking pan. Sift together flour, cocoa, salt and baking powder. Cream butter and sugar in mixing bowl. Add dry ingredients, mixing well. Beat in eggs, corn syrup and vanilla and mix thoroughly. Stir in nuts. Spread in prepared pan and bake 40 to 45 minutes or until center is soft and edges are slightly firm. *Do not overbake.* Let cool completely before frosting and cutting into squares.

Chocolate Frosting

- 2 tablespoons (¼ stick) butter
- 2 ounces unsweetened chocolate
- 2 tablespoons warm water
- 2 teaspoons vanilla
- 2 cups powdered sugar, sifted, then measured
  Walnut halves (optional)

Melt butter and chocolate in top of double boiler over low heat. Blend in water and vanilla. Remove from heat and whisk in powdered sugar until smooth. Spread over completely cooled brownies. Decorate with walnut halves if desired.

Chocolate Spice Cupcakes

Makes 16

- ½ cup vegetable shortening
- 1 cup sugar
- 1 egg
- 1½ teaspoons water
- 1¼ cups sweetened applesauce

- 1½ cups sifted all purpose flour
- ½ cup unsweetened cocoa
- 1¼ teaspoons baking soda
- 1¼ teaspoons cinnamon
- ¼ teaspoon allspice
- ¼ teaspoon freshly grated nutmeg

  Chocolate Frosting (see following recipe)

Preheat oven to 350°F. Fill 16 muffin cups with 2½-inch paper or foil liners.

Place shortening in medium mixing bowl and cream with electric mixer. Beat in sugar, then egg; blend well. Add water and applesauce and beat until batter is well mixed.

Combine sifted flour, cocoa, baking soda, cinnamon, allspice and nutmeg in sifter and mix gently with a spoon, then sift into small mixing bowl. Add sifted ingredients to batter in 3 parts, beating well after each addition. Spoon batter evenly into paper liners. Bake 25 to 30 minutes or until cupcakes spring back when tops are lightly touched with fingers (check at 25 minutes).

Remove cupcakes from cups (but not from paper liners) and cool on wire racks 5 to 10 minutes while you make frosting.

Chocolate Frosting

- 2 tablespoons butter
- ½ cup instant chocolate drink mix
- 2 tablespoons milk
- 1 cup powdered sugar
- ½ teaspoon vanilla

  Candy sprinkles (optional)

Melt butter in small saucepan over low heat, watching carefully so it does not burn. Add chocolate drink mix and milk and stir with wooden spoon until it just begins to bubble; *do not boil*. Remove pan from heat. Add sugar and vanilla and use electric mixer to beat into a smooth frosting. If frosting is too thick, add a bit more milk; if too thin, add a little more sugar.

Immediately spread frosting on warm cupcakes; decorate with candy sprinkles if desired.

Black Bottom Cupcakes

Cream cheese keeps these cupcakes moist and delicious for several weeks.

Makes about 1½ dozen

   8 ounces cream cheese, room temperature
   1 egg
   ⅓ cup sugar
   ⅛ teaspoon salt
   1 cup semisweet chocolate chips

1½ cups all purpose flour
   1 cup sugar
   ¼ cup unsweetened cocoa

1 teaspoon baking soda
½ teaspoon salt
1 cup water
⅓ cup vegetable oil
1 tablespoon white vinegar
1 teaspoon vanilla

Preheat oven to 375°F. Line muffin tins with cupcake papers. Using wooden spoon, blend cream cheese, egg, sugar and salt in mixing bowl. Carefully fold in chocolate chips. Set aside.

Combine dry ingredients in another bowl and mix well. Add remaining ingredients and blend thoroughly. Fill cupcake papers about ¾ full with batter. Drop 1 heaping tablespoonful cream cheese mixture into center of each. Bake until done, 35 to 40 minutes.

6

Ice Cream

Chocolate Sherbet

Makes about 20 ¼-cup
servings

  1¾ cups unsweetened cocoa
   1 cup sugar
  ⅛ teaspoon salt
  3½ cups nonfat milk
      Vanilla bean

Combine cocoa, sugar and salt
in medium saucepan and mix
well. Gradually stir in milk. Split
vanilla bean, scrape out seeds
and add with bean to pan. Place
over medium heat and bring just
to boil, stirring constantly. Reduce heat and simmer, stirring
constantly, 5 minutes. Let cool,
then remove vanilla bean. Pour
into shallow pan and freeze.

Spoon into processor or blender in batches and mix until smooth. Return to freezer if needed or scoop into dishes and serve.

Greatest Chocolate Ice Cream

A superb recipe from France's famous pâtissier, Gaston Lenôtre.

Makes about 1 quart

> 1 cup plus 2 tablespoons half and half
> 1½ ounces unsweetened chocolate
> 6 large egg yolks
> 5½ tablespoons sugar
> 1 cup whipping cream
> 5½ tablespoons sugar
> ¼ cup (½ stick) butter
> ½ teaspoon vanilla

In small heavy-bottomed saucepan combine half and half and chocolate. Stir occasionally to melt chocolate, then slowly bring to boil. Place in refrigerator overnight, or chill in freezer briefly *but do not freeze*.

Cream egg yolks and 5½ table-spoons sugar; set aside.

In 2-quart saucepan combine whipping cream and remaining sugar and slowly bring to boil, stirring frequently.

Add about ⅓ of cream mixture to yolks, whisking constantly. Pour this mixture into saucepan, whisking constantly, and bring to *just under* boiling point. Remove from heat and whisk in butter. Immediately place pan in cold water or over ice to stop cooking. Stir mixture frequently until cool.

Strain through fine strainer or chinoise. Beat in chilled half and half, chocolate and vanilla. Place in ice cream maker and churn according to manufacturer's directions.

Doubled, this recipe will fit into 6-quart ice cream maker.

Rocky Road Ice Cream

Makes about 1 quart

- 1 recipe Greatest Chocolate Ice Cream (see preceding recipe)
- ½ cup semisweet chocolate chips
- ½ cup coarsely chopped toasted almonds or walnuts
- ½ cup miniature marshmallows *or* dark seedless raisins

After ice cream has been churned, fold in chocolate, nuts, and marshmallows or raisins.

7

Sauces and Fondue

Chocolate Sauce

Makes about 1 cup

8 ounces milk chocolate or
  semisweet chocolate
  Whipping cream

Soften chocolate in top of double boiler. Add sufficient cream to achieve desired consistency.

For Mint Chocolate Sauce, add a few drops of mint extract.

Chocolate Marshmallow Sauce

Makes about 2 cups

      6 ounces unsweetened
        chocolate
  1½ cups powdered sugar
      1 cup hot water
      8 large marshmallows or
        ½ cup miniature
      1 teaspoon vanilla

Place all ingredients in heavy-bottomed saucepan and bring to boil, stirring constantly. Remove from heat and continue stirring until chocolate is completely dissolved and mixture thickens. Serve hot or at room temperature.

Chocolate Fondue

12 servings

- 6 ounces unsweetened chocolate
- 1½ cups sugar
- 1 cup whipping cream
- ½ cup (1 stick) butter
- 1½ ounces (3 tablespoons) crème de cacao
  Cake or assorted fruits, cut into bite-size pieces

Combine first 4 ingredients in double boiler over warm water and stir frequently until melted, about 10 minutes. Add crème de cacao and blend mixture well. Serve fondue with cake or assorted fresh fruits.

Index

Credits

The following people contributed the recipes included in this book:

Au Provence, Cleveland Heights, Ohio
Martha Buller
Robert L. Gaines
Bess Greenstone
Zack Hanle
Kirk Huffard
Cyndee Kannenberg
Judy Kostin
Gilda Latzky
Rita Leinwand
Jack Lirio
Helen McCully
Jinx and Jefferson Morgan
Marysol Richwine
Nell Rugee
Shirley Sarvis
Andrea Shapiro
Lari Siler
The Glass Onion, Lawrenceville, New
    Jersey
Webb's Cove, Seabrook, Texas
Jan Weimer
Youngberg's, Arcata, California